Winning the 21ˢᵗ Century

America's new role for a new century

By

Don Nixon

Endorsements

—∿∿∿—

"When far too many of us are ashamed and shackled by the decline we see in American culture, Don Nixon sees an opportunity to fulfill the Great Commission that most of us have missed. Much good can come from using our nation's wealth wisely. This book will open our eyes to the possibilities."

Chuck Gratner, WORD-FM station manager, Pittsburgh, PA

"America already provides the world with more Christian missionaries than any other country. It also happens to produce more wealth than any other country. Coincidence? Don Nixon doesn't think so. At the least, Don sees tremendous possibilities in a joining of these two forces—a possibility to win the 21st century. He has quite a vision to share. Don feels a calling, one that he believes America must heed."

Paul Kengor is an author and Executive Director of the Center for Vision & Values at Grove City College

Jesus said: "...everyone who has been given much, much will be demanded; and from the one who has been entrusted with much, much more will be asked." In the context of this statement what does Jesus require of the USA—the most prosperous nation in the world? In his book *Winning the 21st Century* Don Nixon endeavors to answer this question. In an easy-to-read narrative style Nixon presents a challenge to the USA—that intrinsically tied to their Christian heritage and enormous material blessing is an awesome responsibility— to fund the Great Commission of Jesus Christ. Using helpful anecdotes Nixon explains how the US Christian community is strategically placed to usher in the greatest era of Christian mission this world has ever seen.

David Wraight
President, Youth for Christ International

This effort is dedicated to Shileen;
My wife of twenty-four years.
We have together experienced all that we stated
in our vows:
For richer or poorer, for better or worse.
She has stuck by me through all of it.
For that I am grateful.

And to our sons,
Justin and Austyn.
They have been a source of joy and pride
As we watch them become godly men.

Table of Contents

—∿—

Acknowledgements

—ɱ—

This is a task that is almost certain to ensure that I omit some people. However, I feel the need to give credit to those who played key roles in this effort and those who played less obvious, but to me, vital roles in making this project possible.

First of all, I'd like to thank the members of the Pittsburgh Offensive that provided the crucible for ideas to generate. We spent many Thursdays at Nanky Chalfant's home grappling with various issues and eventually I caught the hint through them from God that this message was necessary and timely. More specifically John Stahl-Wert, President of the Pittsburgh Leadership Foundation, first planted the idea that this message needed to be put into the form of a book.

My thanks also go to Ron Tietz for reviewing the manuscript. Kathryn Van Til provided a professional editing that cleaned up my errors in grammar and structure. They both provided valuable input regarding readability and flow of ideas.

Sylvia Burleigh, from Xulon, was very helpful in walking me through the publishing process.

Many others acted as sounding boards for ideas and gave important feedback and encouragement. They would include Sam Balachander, Stuart Broberg, Chuck Emerson, Dick Epps, Howard Horn, Dennis Hutchison, Bob Lee, Lee Wishing, Phil Nichols and Steve Schaefer. Steve also gave much council in the area of publishing, etc.

There were also mentors and coaches who have greatly influenced me and helped me to discover my passion. Jon Benson, Roy Dayton, Jim Leckie and Forest and Cheryl Townsley were instrumental in helping me muddle through the past several years of self-discovery and transition. (Jim has since gone to meet Jesus face to face.) Other influential mentors from my past include John Bacha (high school football coach), Al Cap (high school gymnastics coach), Wes Lammay (high school YFC/Campus Life Director) and my parents, Sam and Jean Nixon for laying the foundation for all of it.

Joel Smith, my boss and good friend in Youth for Christ, gave me encouragement and allowed the flexibility to take on this project. Many others in YFC have been huge in my life. Dozens of pages would be required to just list names.

Finally, all of you prayer warriors who lift me to the feet of the Creator regularly: specifically Alan Berg (my pastor), Brenda Brenneman, Stuart Broberg and Chuck Emerson and Steve Schaefer (see above), DeeJay and Les Emerson, Marlene and Steve Lipinski, Glenn and Marion Schaefer, Lee Twombly and Jake Tyler.

All of you have a part in this book. I trust that God will be honored by what will be done in peoples' lives as they grapple with the following pages.

Forward

—ᴍ—

It's not the first time that I have received mail from this prestigious law firm in Kansas City, after all, we lived there for twelve years, and I had several contacts that worked for the organization. But when this piece arrived in our home in Denver, it really caught my eye.

In bold copy, the brochure read: "How to transfer your wealth, without transforming your kids." The target audience of the message was the financially successful, and to be fair, the challenge was related to a transfer of wealth to other family members...but the implication of the message caught me squarely, particularly as I was in the middle of reading "Winning the 21st Century". I fundamentally believe just the opposite of the brochure copy that I just related to you. I believe that responsible individuals in this country stand on the threshold of using the wealth that they have accumulated to fund the transformation of young people all over the world...most likely in unprecedented numbers. What a profound and historic opportunity to leverage what God has given to "transform kids" in all contexts and in all situations. Don Nixon provides a personal, pointed and compelling vision of the "what ifs" associated with a mobilization of resources.

As a Baby Boomer myself, I embrace this challenge. I believe that now is the time to move and motivate. In Acts

1:1, Dr. Luke frames his historic report of the explosion of the church by referencing back to the first report he had given in the Gospel of Luke. He refers to it as a report of what Jesus had "begun" to do. What Jesus ignited during his personal ministry, we have the opportunity to continue in powerful and exponential ways. He made it clear that his ministry, and the church in general, were just getting started. I believe that with all my heart, and believe that the time is now to make sure that we heed the call to invest in the transformation of the next generation. What a profound opportunity awaits us.

Dan Wolgemuth
President-Youth for Christ/USA

Introduction

—〰—

There are times when you just can't put it down. Times you can't walk away from it. This is just such a time. God has given me just such a message.

Occasionally, I have been uncertain that He is speaking to me. At times, I have been hesitant to pursue this, wondering, "is this really a God-message?" But He has kept bringing me back to it again and again for the past several years.

Over the past thirty-plus years I have been involved in taking the life-changing message of Jesus Christ to lost teenagers through the ministry of Youth for Christ. It is the most important message and responsibility that exist today. Whether it's one-on-one, a weekly meeting or a large event I have had the privilege of delivering that vital and urgent message in all of those settings and more. <u>Only now has another issue arisen, that for me, commands equal urgency</u>.

Our nation is at a crossroads. We've been at these types of intersections before—the American Revolution, the Civil War and slavery are among the major issues we have faced. In the twentieth century alone we headed into two world wars, a depression and several other crucial events (not to mention cultural and family issues). 9-11 is the latest of those defining moments. In spite of all of these severe crises, the United States is still the wealthiest, most prosperous nation in all of history. Therein lie the message and the challenge.

There is no way that we are at this level of prosperity and world leadership because we are lucky or even because we are simply highly blessed by God. There has to be more to it—like a designed plan and/or a sense of calling as a nation. That means we have a God-given purpose. We have fulfilled that purpose in many ways in our history, but that purpose is also dynamic—it changes as the times and needs of the world change. I believe this new century is inaugurating a time of unprecedented significance concerning our role as a nation.

With all of my heart, I believe that <u>our role as American Christians for the twenty-first century is to finance the Great Commission</u>. The Great Commission is the assignment that Jesus gave His followers right before he ascended from the planet. We are to take His message into the entire world. That takes resources these days. The United States has more of that than anyone.

There are two reasons why I believe God has given us this huge role. First, we have a <u>unique Christian heritage</u> that no other country can match—especially regarding our founding. Second, we are <u>the wealthiest nation on Earth</u>. I don't believe any of that is by accident. Those two factors are intricately woven together as part of the fabric of this land and it all <u>screams out our responsibility</u>. It is called Winning the 21st Century!

That may beg the question—"Who is this guy and what qualifies him to make this kind of proclamation?" First, I will not pretend to be more than an amateur historian. Therefore, this is not a work brimming with scholarship. That's not my purpose here. My knowledge of our nation's Christian heritage comes from a deep interest and passion of how God has worked throughout our history. For all of my adult years I have been reading, studying, listening and going to historic sites. I've been to Gettysburg several times, Antietam, Manassas, Valley Forge, Washington's Crossing of the Delaware River, Brandywine, Mount Vernon, Ford's Theater, Independence Hall, Lexington and Concord, Plymouth Rock, Yorktown, The Alamo, St. Augustine, Fort Necessity, Fort Ticonderoga, Jamestown, Williamsburg and many places in Washington, D.C. just to name a few. I could easily be a History Channel addict. A dream vacation for me would be visiting battlefields for a week. (Haven't been able to sell that one to the family yet.) I always stop at roadside markers. Dates of historic events stick to my brain. In other words, I have a fascination and sense of call concerning our historical and spiritual roots.

The context of this history is that it is all in the hands of God. We can either go where God wants to take us or we can resist and simply indulge our own desires with this unprecedented wealth. The former raises us to a spectacular level of godly service and character. The latter causes us to spiral down to the depths of myopic materialism and eventually nihilism. We have plenty of examples of both results in our culture. It is a <u>great and awesome responsibility to be entrusted with all of this prosperity</u>. It all comes down to stewardship and God will hold us accountable for how we handled it. See the parable of the talents (Matthew 25:14-30). The United States has been entrusted with much.

Secondly, as I said above, I haven't been able to put this aside. Next to my family, the two great passions in my life are reaching lost people and discovering our Christian heritage as a nation. Somehow, God led me to wed the two and this book was born out of that process.

There is one other point that I think is very critical in this whole picture. History is important. The shame is that, to many students, it is the most boring of subjects. The sentiment often is, "memorizing dates is irrelevant, anything that happened before I was born doesn't matter and who cares what a bunch of dead guys in powdered wigs had to say over two hundred years ago."

The bigger shame is that history teaches us that we learn nothing from history. What a pathetic commentary on our generation!

The truth is that reality television shows like Survivor, The Amazing Race and others capture the attention and imagination of millions of viewers. All they are seeing is history in the making—and it's not even at all consequential on an historic level. The stories that are consequential are riveting in their drama and significance. George Washington crossing the Delaware River with a few thousand troops in horrendous weather, marching eight miles in the middle of the night and then surprising the Hessian soldiers at Christmas in 1776 after losing battles for the previous eighteen months is absolutely legendary. <u>No way is it boring</u>! Too few of our population know any of these stories. American history reads like an Indiana Jones adventure—the action never stops. Our nation's history has an abundance of people who have overcome great odds, done the heroic and made the impossible comeback.

All of this brings us to our purpose as a nation today and what role we each play. History is great but for what reason has our Christian heritage laid a foundation? It's good to know our spiritual roots but what do we do with it? On the other hand, telling people to be more generous with their wealth is not very motivating. Either piece alone is incomplete. They must be married together to create the compelling rationale for us to answer our God-given call. And answer that call we must.

Chapter 1

Winning a Century?

—𝔪—

What in the world does it mean to win a century? Moreover, why should any of us even care? A century is longer than most of us will live and only the youngest among our population will ever see 2099. Is there any possible way for our minds to grasp such a huge chunk of history? We are, in many ways, just beginning to understand the ramifications of the 20th century. How can we strategically look at the 21st century and feel at all qualified to make any plans <u>for our own lives</u>, let alone think of impacting a nation, or much less the world for the next 100 years? Maybe this is too overwhelming!

It would be too overwhelming except for the fact that the last thing Jesus told us to do before he left this earth was "Go into all the world and preach the good news to all creation." (Mark 16:15 NIV) You know the rest. Our assignment is to transform the planet. He said he would give us the tools to do so. Acts 1:8 states, "You will receive power when the Holy Spirit comes on you; and you will be my witnesses in Jerusalem, and in all Judea and Samaria, and to the ends of the earth." That includes everywhere. We haven't been given the option to exclude anybody or to strictly localize our efforts.

We are now in the early years of a new century. Rarely has a new century been demarcated so dramatically as has this twenty-first. September 11, 2001 saw to that. Everything that now happens in our world is seen through the lens of that event. It has changed every day of our lives, even if in very subtle ways. Thus, it is fitting that we look at our role as Christians, and more specifically, as American Christians in this new post 9-11 world. I believe our role has changed—and should change—in light of recent events. When I say "recent" I mean in terms of history—say the last couple of decades or so. 9-11 was just one of several critical pieces to the puzzle regarding where we should focus our efforts in the years to come. That will be explored.

A century may seem to be a random time period to focus on, but there's something about that big number flipping that seems significant. It's like going over 100,000 miles on your car. It's a milestone.

Even though 100 years is a huge chunk of time, there have often been nations and even people who have dominated their century. Just a few examples would include:

- **The Roman Empire of the first century**—Actually Rome dominated much longer than just 100 years, but the peak of their empire was around the time of Jesus Christ.
- **Spain in the 1500s**—That was their golden era for exploration and conquering. They eventually ruled most of the Americas except for the east coast of what is now the USA, where the English colonies were developed starting in 1607. The French had also colonized some of what we now know as Canada. Other than that Spain controlled most of the Western Hemisphere. England pretty much ended their dominance by defeating the Spanish Armada in 1588.
- **England in the 1800s**—Talk about an empire! "The sun never sets on the British Empire." How true that

was! Great Britain controlled much of Africa, India, Australia and many other places around the world. Fortunately many of these colonies were able to obtain independence without a war. It didn't usually work that way with Spain.

- **The Reformation of the 1500s**—This movement started earlier with many who began to blaze the trail but was really launched with the likes of Martin Luther, John Calvin, John Knox, and many others who genuinely reshaped the Christian world. The results of this seminal event are many and include the founding of the United States.

Of course, we could mention the dominance of the United States in the 20th century. That will be addressed later. On a more personal level each one of us is at the crossroads of at least 200 years of family history. Our lives will affect not only our children, but our grandchildren and great-grandchildren as well. That easily reaches 100 years into the future for most of us. It also means we are affected for good or for bad by what our great-grandparents did. For me that spans from the last few decades of the 1800s all the way into the 22nd century—well over 200 years.

We should never think that looking at an entire century is too encompassing. How we live will impact those who will come after us—even those born to our grandchildren.

In light of all of this, it's very timely to investigate what our role might be as American Christians in this sure-to-be-tumultuous new century.

Chapter 2

What a way to begin a century!

—∽∞∾—

The cell phone rang. We had a pretty good idea who it was and we were right. My wife Shileen heard her worried mother implore us to turn back and go home. I told her, "We're in the middle of nowhere. This is the safest place we could be. Nobody's gonna come after us here."

Such was my response while driving on the Pennsylvania Turnpike with my family. We were headed to Ocean City, NJ to meet with other staff to plan next year's summer trip for the Eastern Region of Youth for Christ. We could expect nearly 1000 teenagers and staff to be part of this annual event that had been taking place since the 1950s. We kept updating the program with cutting edge music, speakers and technology. It was a powerful time each year in the lives of the many young people who attended.

I took the family along since we could sneak in some fun time at the beach and boardwalk, as the crowds would be way down from the peak of summer. It was September. Kids back in school. We'll have the place to ourselves! And since we home schooled our two boys we had the flexibility to do this.

For us a drive to the oceanfront is at least seven hours. An opportunity to be there is prime. We took off a little before

8:00am from our home near Pittsburgh and headed east. The anticipation was evident—even with a family that had only one "morning person" (that would be me). About an hour or so into our travels I flipped on the radio to catch the news at 9. Until that moment September 11, 2001 was just the next day on the calendar. That was about to change.

The first report was that a small plane had hit the World Trade Center. A little later we heard that it might be a passenger airliner. Soon the word came that the second tower was hit. At that instant I knew we were under attack. There is no way there would be two accidents at both towers that close together in time. The newscast would not make that speculation for quite some time, but there was no doubt as far as I was concerned. That conviction was driven deeper as we caught the news of the Pentagon being hit a little later as well. This was a planned and deliberate attack on America—not just some random terrorists executing their own personal jihad.

We were all glued to the radio for the rest of the trip. It was frustrating to not have a TV available. We didn't see any video until late that afternoon when we arrived at our room. Meanwhile, my sons (at the time Justin was 13 and Austyn was 8) asked me why I was getting angry. I muttered something about "those filthy maggots" and other strong language while narrowly avoiding actual profanity. I also hoped out loud that God would turn hell up a few thousand degrees for the terrorists' reception. I hated hearing all of this but neither could I turn it off. I had to see what was happening to the country that I love.

Little did we know that United Flight 93 was about to plunge into the earth at 500 miles per hour not too far from where we were near Somerset, PA. Maybe my mother-in-law was right.

Throughout the next few days as we continued to plan this Youth for Christ event, I could tell the world would never be the same. It was fascinating to be close enough to New York City to pick up on their radio broadcasts. The continual coverage and commentary reinforced the "no turning back" feel this all had. One incident stands out and it'll forever feel like it happened just yesterday. I was driving alone at one point on Thursday (Sept. 13) when Lee Greenwood's song "God Bless the USA" began to play. That alone was a powerful moment, moving me at a deep level as I thought about what kind of future may be ahead of us. Halfway through the song a tricked-out, lift-kit-enhanced pick-up truck came by with a monster American flag staked in its bed and totally unfurled in the wind. That did it. The emotional floodgates blew open and I started crying, yelling and pounding my fist on the dash—"NO WAY CAN THEY BEAT US! NO WAY!!" I absolutely knew we would rise to the occasion as one, confront this threat and win.

The next day (Friday) the staff and I were finished with our work and our family decided to add an extra day to the trip. We were only a couple of hours from New York and besides—history was being made. On the way we saw more American flags than I've ever seen. They were on houses, cars, hanging from bridges, suspended between two cranes at a construction site, etc., etc. Even before crossing from New Jersey over to Staten Island, we could see the smoke that was off in the distance. Little by little we moved closer and often would catch a glimpse of the Statue of Liberty and the smoke plume that marked the now former twin towers. As fortune would have it (or God's providence in my book), we became stuck in traffic in Brooklyn right across the East River from Ground Zero with a perfect view of the site—at least as perfect as it could be with all the smoke. Soon we were moving again and eventually crossed over into Manhattan.

We parked and moved as close as we could which was at least ten blocks or so away from the site. It was sobering but fascinating to see all the shrines with candles burning and pictures of missing loved ones posted all over that part of town. Every one of those faces represented several if not hundreds of family, friends and co-workers who were at least very concerned and at most worried-sick about the fate of these missing people. At this point it was still a rescue operation as they were hoping to find some folks yet alive. Emergency vehicles moved to and from the site on a continual basis and were always cheered by the crowd. At about that same time President Bush was at Ground Zero to encourage the workers. However, all we could see was smoke as we looked down the many blocks in that direction. The amount of dust was incredible—all over buildings, cars, trees, everything.

Eventually we got in the car and started up toward Midtown Manhattan. We knew that all of the southern part of the island was not business as usual, but there was still activity and people moving around. As we headed north, we saw a stretch of about fifteen to twenty blocks that was totally deserted. It was an eerie feeling driving a mile or two through the nation's largest city in the middle of the day—and not seeing anybody! Did we miss the Second Coming? As we got closer to Midtown, the activity level began to pick up. When we hit Times Square it was the usual New York City hustle and bustle.

You know, I'm quite comfortable with city driving, but this place gave me some experiences I never get in Pittsburgh. I remember waiting at a red light and watching up ahead as a guy worked his car into a parallel parking space. I saw the car in front of him jump, then the car behind him jumped. The car in front jumped again, then the car behind—this process repeating itself several times. He was creating a space from one that was about a foot shorter than what he wanted. Soon the car was nestled in just right. When the light turned green and we drove by, I saw a vehicle that looked like it was the project for ball-peen hammer day in shop class. It looked like he was a veteran of this parking technique. What did he care—he got his space!

Soon we were heading across the George Washington Bridge and out of New York City. There was plenty of drive time to reflect on what this event would mean to a country that was still in triage with an open wound. What a way to begin a century!

Chapter 3

Defining Moments

—⟋⟍—

Why the personal story about September 11? It illustrates how and why a defining moment has the impact that it does. It changes nearly everything. We think differently, we view the world differently and we operate differently on a day-to-day basis, even if in just subtle ways.

Do you have a period of time or event in your life that you would consider to be a "defining moment?" I can think of at least six times in my life that had such an impact that my life would never be the same again. Most of these were not single events but periods of massive change that lasted anywhere from several weeks to a few years. For me the ages of 5, 14, 19, 27, 36 and 44 all had that can-never-go-back feel to them. Some of the times were difficult, some just ushered in major change. All of them were used by God to prepare me for what He had planned next. For instance at age five we moved into a new home in a new community. I made new friends and the next year started school—huge change—but all very positive. At fourteen I had one of my best friends move away, started into the brand new just-built high school and got involved with Campus Life (a ministry of Youth for Christ that reaches out to high school students) where I soon committed my life to Christ. Life changed radically again—mostly for the good.

The tough one, but probably the most defining one came at age nineteen while a freshman at the University of Pittsburgh. I walked on to the football team at the beginning of the school year. (A walk-on has no scholarship but can try to make the team.) Since I had a good high school career and several scholarship offers to smaller schools, I figured I'd give it a shot. There's a whole testimony to this story, but basically that was the period when Pitt brought in a new coach and he took the team that had one win and ten losses in 1972 to an undefeated national championship in four years. I was caught up in the transition with spring football drills in 1973 as he began to rebuild the team. I was also subsequently cut after the Spring Game and was devastated. To make matters worse, I was put on academic probation that semester (too much dedication to football) and cut my hand severely in a lawn mower accident—all within a few weeks. As I lay in the hospital bed viewing a life that I thought was in ruins, God was using this to refine me for the next chapter. That summer I got involved again with Campus Life and my life took a radically different direction as I eventually joined the staff of Youth for Christ in Washington, PA. Through that involvement over the last thirty-plus years, God used me to change more lives than I could ever hope to do playing football. What I thought was ruin God turned into gold.

Most of us have an event or events that divide history into distinct eras. It can be personal or historical events. Everything that happened before that event and everything that happens after it are seen as different eras. Things like the death of a family member, serious illness or major career change are among those that provide that dividing line on a personal level. For older folks the Depression and/or World War II provide that dividing line historically. Later on it became the assassination of President John F. Kennedy in 1963. For most of us today it's 9-11. Everything that happened before 9-11 is seen from a different perspective compared to all that has happened and will happen since that defining moment. The fact that it happened at the beginning of a new century merely underscores the change.

I believe that the same dynamic is at work with us corporately as Americans. Look at how life has changed since September 11, 2001. Most of us go on with our lives and it may look like business as usual. However, on September 10, 2001, terms such as terrorist, World Trade Center, Taliban, Al Qaeda, Osama bin-Laden and suicide bomber occupied little or no disk space in our cranial hard drives. Today they're in our daily discourse and every newscast. We have a world that is morphing into who knows what and we are straining to understand our nation's role in these volatile times.

So just what is our role as a nation in this frightful new century of global terrorism and other issues we never dreamed about just a few short years ago? I have invested countless hours of brainpower and discussion in this arena of thought. There are a few ideas that have surfaced that I believe merit a closer look.

We all want our lives to have meaning and purpose. That is how we are created. We want to know that our relationships, our work, our time and our energy matter for something—that all of our daily blur of activities aren't just keeping us busy until our expiration date. I believe it's the same with a nation. When we have a sense of purpose, we feel good about contributing to the welfare of that nation. It makes all the work and sacrifice significant.

I'm convinced that God has a purpose for our nation. Yeah, I know—WOW! Big news flash! So have millions of others. Terms like "Manifest Destiny" have been part of the American lexicon throughout our history. Now I'm not suggesting that the United States is the "new Israel" as some claim, but I do believe God has raised this nation up for His specific purposes. However, I believe <u>that our role in that larger purpose has changed in just the last several years.</u> This doesn't necessarily tie directly to 9-11, but the timing is interesting. 9-11 has forced us to re-examine our place in a whole new world that is the 21st century.

I believe a major role that God has for our nation in the 21st century is the <u>funding of His</u> <u>Great Commission.</u> No other country could take on this role for a number of reasons. The rest of this book is dedicated to making the case as to why I hold this to be true.

First we need some historical perspective in order to understand this changing purpose.

Chapter 4

A Totally Unique Birth

—⌇⌇—

The birth of our nation was a miracle—actually a series of many miracles and various acts of Providence. Some things did not seem supernatural at the time, but the hand of God was most present. In biblical history consider the situation of Joseph being sold into slavery but God using that to save his entire family and ultimately the nation of Israel. Throughout history there were times when circumstances looked horribly grim but as Joseph stated, "...God intended it for good to accomplish what is now being done." (Gen. 50:20 NIV)

A great example from American history would be how the Pilgrims came to settle in New England in 1620 as opposed to Virginia. They originally intended to land the Mayflower near the Hudson River (present day New York City), the northern-most part of the Virginia colony that was established with the founding of Jamestown in 1607. Storms had blown them north to Cape Cod and it would be very dangerous to try to go back south, so they settled at Plymouth. It was very difficult in many ways with the approaching winter, being out of the jurisdiction and protection of the Virginia Charter and having no known person to greet them. It was to be a brand new start.

The Pilgrims met a Native American who surprisingly spoke English quite well. British explorers several years earlier had kidnapped Squanto and he eventually made his way back home with a new language and a new faith in the true God. He was a huge aid to the Pilgrims regarding food and relations with the indigenous population. In addition, by being outside the boundaries of the Virginia Charter they had to come up with their own government. That resulted in the Mayflower Compact.

The "misfortune" of landing off course can now be seen as the hand of God through the eyes of perspective. It placed an English speaking, godly colony of believers in a new area that would ultimately become part of the United States. As a result the colonies spread farther north than might have otherwise occurred. They formed a government that was a model for many to follow as subsequent colonies came into being.

The events that took place surrounding the American Revolution (1775-83) and the drafting of the Constitution (1787) were only possible because of favorable circumstances, brilliant and godly founders that prayed, tremendous natural resources and great timing being among the factors. Was all of this just good luck or was God orchestrating the development of this nation? Now I'm not one who claims that everything America did was right and everything the British did was wrong regarding the Revolution. It's definitely more complex than that. There were (and still are) many believers that suggest that there was not enough cause to rebel against England since the colonies did experience a high degree of freedom and were not really oppressed. (Although the clamps were tightened more and more in the 1770s with increasing numbers of British troops installed in the colonies.) However, no matter what your theology or opinion of the Revolution, the birthing of the USA was an unprecedented phenomenon.

When George Washington was appointed commander of the Continental Army in 1775, nobody could have anticipated the number of battles that would be lost in order to win the war. He basically led his army on a series of retreats over the next eighteen months while up against the most powerful military force in the world. Starting in the summer of 1775 in Boston, they fell back to New York City, New Jersey and eventually Pennsylvania before Washington made the bold move of crossing the Delaware River on Christmas night of 1776. He marched through the night and defeated the Hessian mercenaries in Trenton, New Jersey. That victory helped turn an important corner in the American Revolution.

However, that opportunity might never have arrived if his army had been wiped out the previous summer in New York City. On August 27, 1776, the British Army trapped the Continental Army of 8,000 men against the East River at Brooklyn Heights. They were vastly outnumbered. This was looking very ugly for a fledgling nation that just declared itself independent the previous month. General Washington made a daring decision to cross the mile-wide river at night to escape to Manhattan. Many skilled fishermen and mariners ensured that this move was done as quietly as possible since it was right under the nose of British ships. It was all the more amazing since cannons and other military equipment were saved as well. By morning they still had about three hours of transporting troops to go and that with the loss of darkness for cover. Major Benjamin Tallmadge's unit was still to be evacuated when, as he wrote, "At this time, a very dense fog began to rise out of the ground and off the river, and it seemed to settle in a peculiar manner over both encampments. I recollect this providential occurrence perfectly well, and so very dense was the atmosphere that I could scarcely discern a man at six-yard distance....We tarried until the sun had risen, but the fog remained as dense as ever." As the fog lifted, the British came to find the trenches empty. They fired on the last boats to leave, but the Patriots were just out of range. This gave them time to regroup in Manhattan and basically continue the retreat intact.

Even after the victory in Trenton and a few other wins for Washington and his army, they still had to confront other losses and then Valley Forge for the winter of 1777-78. There were key wins in other parts of the new nation—namely Saratoga in New York, Monmouth in New Jersey and in the southern colonies. Certainly much of the credit goes to the French for eventually siding with us. There is also the fact that this drawn out conflict took its toll on British resources with all the other activity they had to deal with throughout their empire.

The war finally ended when Washington and the French Navy had British General Cornwallis surrounded at Yorktown, Virginia in September of 1781. There was probably never another time when an army lost so many battles and yet won the war. Even so, it still wasn't officially over until the Treaty of Paris in 1783.

That same year General Washington made another stunning move. He voluntarily resigned his commission as Commander-in-Chief of the Continental Army. This is the General Washington that could have become King George of the United States. He was just about the most famous person in the world and was most responsible for the victory over the British during the Revolution. He was, at this time, easily the most powerful person in our young country. Throughout history generals would conquer and then rule. Washington knew that a military regime was not the way to start this nation. He knew that civilian rule was the preferred path, so he stepped down of his own free will. Of course, he was elected four years later (1787) as President of the Constitutional Convention and in 1789 was unanimously elected as our first President. He still ended up on top but in a fashion that best served his country—as an elected official. Nonetheless, he also voluntarily resigned the Presidency after serving two terms. Again, he could have served for life if he had wanted to do so. That chosen course of limiting his time in office set a precedent that was not broken until Franklin Roosevelt won a third term in 1940. (In 1951 the 22ⁿᵈ Amendment of the Constitution was ratified. It limited to two the number of terms to which a person could be elected President.)

How often do you have the opportunity to create a nation from scratch? For thousands of years there were kingdoms that were passed down from generation to generation. This could go on for centuries or possibly a coup would take place or an invading army would seize control. One way or another, it's just the next despot with a bigger sword. On the other hand, when you study the approximately 250 founders of this nation (including their intellectual and spiritual capital), the times that existed in the late 18ᵗʰ century, the protection from invasion that the Atlantic Ocean afforded, the vast resources (most of which were not even known yet), one can only conclude that the conditions were about as good as it gets to design and build a nation. Was this the hand of God or just a bunch of circumstances that happened to be well aligned? Too many coincidences took place for this to be developing by chance only.

God makes it clear that history serves His purposes. However, many believe that:

- History is just a series of ups and downs, war and peace, etc., etc. In other words history is cyclical. We may do things more high-tech these days, but the principle events of life still run in cycles. Whatever we've seen we'll see again. There's nothing really new.
- Or, history is chaotic. There is no rhyme or reason to events. We are carried along by a bunch of circumstances and there's not a lot we can do about it.

The truth is that history is going some place—it has a goal. Some have said that history is just His Story. Jesus Christ is the culmination of history. That does not mean we just go along for the ride. He has given us an assignment—the Great Commission. We are to be all about that effort. That is true for all believers, but what about the United States in particular? More specifically, what about the believers that live in America?

Looking back again, what were these never-before-seen moves that involved our founding all about? What purpose would this new nation serve?

Chapter 5

The U.S.A. Grows Up

—∾∾—

For the next several decades there was plenty of doubt as to whether this "American Experiment" of government by the people would ever work. However, there were some signs that it would:

- In 1794 President Washington sent troops to put down the Whiskey Rebellion in southwestern Pennsylvania. It was the first time the new government used federal forces to deal with what many thought was a state issue. Controversial as it was, it did help to establish the viability of the new nation in a time when most citizens were loyal to their state way before they were to the United States.

- Democratic-Republican Thomas Jefferson defeated Federalist incumbent John Adams in the Presidential election of 1800. It was our first time for the opposition to come to power, thus providing a real test of the Constitution. Throughout history this process would involve a violent coup or even civil war. It was done, not without political maneuvering and wrangling, but without bloodshed.

There were other signs that did not bode so well:

- Many of our founders went to their graves without assurance that this nation would succeed. This had never been tried before and it would be many decades before anyone knew whether a population could indeed govern themselves. In the words of John Adams, "We have no government armed with power capable of contending with human passions unbridled by morality and religion. Avarice, ambition, revenge or gallantry would break the strongest cords of our Constitution as a whale goes through a net. Our Constitution is designed only for a moral and religious people. It is wholly inadequate for any other." Adams felt strongly that what chance we had could only be had by people with a strong spiritual foundation.

- We fought a second war with England (1812-14) to illustrate that we were not yet fully functional as an independent entity. There were residual disputes from three or four decades earlier regarding territory, etc.

Something began to happen soon after that. Westward expansion grew the nation and we became stronger with each passing year. States were added to the original thirteen on a regular basis from Vermont (the 14th) in 1791 to California (the 31st) in 1850 and eventually everywhere in between. Our adolescent chutzpah made us think that anything was possible. The Industrial Revolution took hold and we became a mature adult as the 19th century progressed. The major blight on our record was slavery, which required a costly civil war to end. After that there was no stopping us. The combination of seemingly unlimited land, abundant natural resources, government and economic systems that were entrepreneur-friendly and a steady wave of willing-to-work immigrants fueled a juggernaut.

We entered the 20th century as a world power and it has been appropriately dubbed "The American Century." There are many reasons for this moniker. Most of the world in 1900 was made up of kingdoms and dictatorships. The relatively few republics were mostly in Europe and the Western Hemisphere. By 2000 most of the world had some form of elected government. The United States played a huge, if not the major, role in that transformation. When you consider the fact that democratically elected governments rarely, if ever, go to war with each other, the United States may have been instrumental in preventing many conflicts in the 20ᵗʰ century. Nations that are strong trading partners are not as likely to battle each other. Oppression and war have been the trademarks of monarchies and dictatorships.

Economically our model has been exported as well. Most nations now recognize private property rights as opposed to everything being controlled by the state, the monarch or a few land barons. We also played major, if not dominant, roles in two world wars and the Cold War. Much could be said about any of these topics. Suffice it to say that the United States' role on the world stage in the 20ᵗʰ century was nothing short of overwhelming. But it was our influence, not our domination that made the difference in the world. Ronald Reagan often quoted Pope Pius XII who was Pope from 1939 until 1958: "Into the hands of America, God has placed an afflicted mankind" and "The American people have a genius for splendid and unselfish action."

Now we enter the 21ˢᵗ century as the world's only "Superpower," a status that some are less than comfortable with since there is no "counterbalance" like the Soviet Union, but it is what it is. What will we have to offer our planet in this brave new century? Nobody can know what the world will look like when 12-31-2099 turns over to 1-1-2100. Many believe this century will be China's time with their exploding economy, although at this point China's gross domestic product (GDP) is only a fraction of what the United States generates. China also has other issues that will have a serious impact on its ability to compete in the future. Although it does have a market driven economy to a large degree, they still have a repressive government that puts the clamps on politics and culture. On one hand, they are building infrastructure the size of Houston every thirty days. On the other hand, China has 150,000,000 men with no prospect of marriage. The culture that favors boys and the government's one child policy has become a formula for disaster. The surplus of single men is building this overabundance of infrastructure, but eventually there will be a shortage of workers to sustain it. There has been a government campaign with ads stating that girls are good. It's a tough call to predict what China's prospects are in the long term.

Many observers believe that India is the sleeper that has the best shot at giving the United States an economic challenge down the road. Their strong family structure and increasingly higher educated population are a powerful combination. Indian people, by and large, also have a great work ethic. How many times do you call customer service for any reason and find an Indian accent greeting you on the other end? Not only did they learn the job, they also learned English and are likely working in the middle of the night to take your call. In addition, being the largest republic in the world provides the atmosphere for all of these strengths to thrive. In any case, both China and India have populations that exceed one billion people. That will be a major factor in the 21ˢᵗ century.

We can never say for certain that our nation is destined to be the lead dog in perpetuity. Nonetheless, I'm certain that the United States will play a huge role in the world for the foreseeable future in political as well as economic terms. That may not, however, be the most important way in which we contribute to the welfare of the globe.

The other angle from which we need to look upon our role as a nation is the spiritual one. We have the God-given foundation and heritage to make our strongest and most important contribution in this twenty-first century be one that changes millions of lives forever. Financing the Great Commission will generate a more powerful impact on Planet Earth than anything we could possibly do in the political or military realm. That doesn't mean the political and military factors are not important. They just pale in significance to the potential that we are sitting on right now to reach a lost world and hasten the return of the King of kings. The next few chapters spell out why and how.

I do not believe that we have developed the richest nation in history just to bless ourselves and then race to see who can die with the most toys. Our prosperity is a result of a Christian heritage and work ethic, and should be directed toward blessing others. That requires a right condition of the heart. As you read on, I trust you'll discover how blessed we are as a nation and then how rewarding it can be to become a conduit of that blessing.

Chapter 6

Roots and Revival

—m—

This idea that our country has Christian roots goes at least all the way back to 1620 and the Pilgrims, but you can make the case that even Christopher Columbus was led by God in his journey to "discover America" in 1492. I realize that Mr. Columbus has taken his lumps in our world of political correctness. He was a man of his times and did many things that would raise more than a few eyebrows today. On the other hand, his personal diary records the motivation for his explorations: (to) "bring the Gospel of Jesus Christ to the heathens" and (to) "bring the Word of God to unknown coastlands." Even with all of his foibles and those of the many who would follow, you can see that God was orchestrating the events that would form America.

The Mayflower Compact was signed on November 11, 1620, by forty-one of our forefathers and is considered by some to be the "birth certificate" of America. This document was to establish how the Pilgrims would be governed in the new world. It is only one page in length but opens in this fashion: "Having undertaken, for the glory of God and advancement of the Christian Faith and Honour of our King and Country, a Voyage to plant the First Colony in the Northern Parts of Virginia...." Thus the first line of the first document from the occupants of the Mayflower establishes the tone for our nation to be formed 156 years later. There is no mention of conquering the land. They were here for religious freedom and to live before God as they saw fit. That would include taking the Gospel to the native people but not subjugating them. That ideal was violated immensely at times in the future, but the proper foundation was laid.

The British colonies grew to thirteen spanning the eastern seaboard from New England to Georgia (which was the last of the original thirteen, gaining its charter in 1733). As the colonies matured, many people continued to arrive for opportunity, political freedom and religious freedom. They developed their economies, cultures and governments, living for the most part as if they were a sovereign nation—or a cluster of smaller ones. There wasn't much interference from the mother country. It wasn't until the 1760's that the seeds of independence began to sprout due to taxation.

Events such as The Great Awakening (late 1730s to early 1740s) kept the people spiritually quickened. This revival had taken up the mantle from Puritanism that had lost its clout with the people. It broke out in New England and spread through the land. The movement has been compared to the radicalism of the 1960s. The emotional outbursts and new religious experiences seemed to create as much controversy as support. A big issue was the "raised affections" vs. the "enlightened mind" that many feared was not the way men should respond to the Gospel. Jonathan Edwards, a leading figure (as was George Whitefield) in this revival, insisted that a religion of the heart was healthy. He did caution that good feelings are not always signs of grace. In any case, the spiritual condition of this pre-natal nation continued to develop.

Our colonial days were also the period when the first colleges were founded. Believe it or not there was a time when we had nothing but Christian colleges. The first institutions of higher learning (now Ivy League schools) were all established and built on the foundation of Christ. In fact, almost every Ivy League school was started primarily to train ministers of the gospel. Their founders wanted to evangelize the Atlantic seaboard! Let's check the record:

- **Harvard, 1636.** Just sixteen years after the Pilgrims set foot in the New World at Plymouth, the Puritans (highly educated people) founded Harvard. According to the school's own archives: "After God had carried us safely to New England, and we had built our houses, provided necessaries for our livelihood, reared convenient places for God's worship, and settled the civil government; one of the next things we longed for, and looked after was to advance learning, and perpetuate it to posterity; dreading to leave an illiterate ministry to the churches, when our present ministers shall lie in the dust." Harvard's "Rules and Precepts" (1646) included the following: "Every one shall consider the main end of his life and studies to know God and Jesus Christ which is eternal life....Every one shall so exercise himself in reading the Scriptures twice a day that they be ready to give an account of their proficiency therein, both in theoretical observations of languages and logic, and in practical and spiritual truths..." Fifty-two percent of Harvard's graduates in the seventeenth century became ministers.
- **Yale, 1701.** Christians in Connecticut thought that an alternative to Harvard was needed due to distance, cost, and that the spiritual climate was not what it once had been.
- **Princeton, 1746.** This former "College of New Jersey" came about as a result of the First Great Awakening and retained its evangelical flavor longer than any Ivy League school. Presidents that were evangelical Christians led Princeton at least until the

turn of the twentieth century. Many faculty members were of the same spiritual persuasion.

- **Dartmouth, 1754.** This school was launched in a strong missionary thrust with the intent of reaching Indian tribes as well as English youth.
- **Columbia, William and Mary, Brown and Rutgers** are also among those that were founded by Christians. The University of Pennsylvania (Penn) was the only college founded before the American Revolution by other than some branch of the Christian church.

Another telling sign is the references to God in the colonial charters and eventually their state constitutions that followed. All of the colonies were founded on the precepts of Christianity and their founding documents state as much. A few examples:

- **Pennsylvania**—The colonial legislature in a 1705-06 act required that civil magistrates had to "also profess to believe in Jesus Christ, the savior of the world." The 1790 state constitution affirms "that no person, who acknowledges the being of God, and a future state of rewards and punishments, shall, on account of his religious sentiments, be disqualified to hold any office or place of trust or profit under this commonwealth."
- **Massachusetts**—Its state constitution of 1780 upholds these qualifications for holding office: "No person shall be eligible to this office, unless...he shall declare himself to be of the Christian religion."
- **North Carolina**—The 1776 state constitution specifies these qualifications for public office: "No person who shall deny the being of God, or the truth of the Protestant religion, or the divine authority of the Old or New Testaments, or who shall hold religious principles incompatible with the freedom and safety of

the State, shall be capable of holding any office or place of trust or profit in the civil department within this state." This provision was in place until 1876.

Again, I believe God's hand was evident during these times. By 1776 there were less than three million colonists. The religious make-up included 99% Protestant, 1% Catholic and 0.1% Jewish. That set the tone for the period that included the American Revolution and the drafting of the Constitution.

It's fascinating to think that religious freedom never really existed before the time of the Constitution. In virtually every nation there was a state religion. Other faiths were frowned upon or even persecuted. England probably came the closest with the greatest degree of tolerance, but it still was not true religious freedom.

After the Revolution Christianity actually experienced a decline. As the frontier expanded many Christian leaders noted decay in the morality of the settlers. Many of these leaders observed rampant alcoholism, land grabbing and the "prevalence of vice and infidelity" a frontier Presbytery noted in its minutes. The increasing popularity of universalism (doctrine that all will be saved) and deism (belief that God is uninvolved in the world) was also of great concern. The Methodist Church, the most popular denomination among middle and lower classes, actually declined in membership between 1794 and 1799. In the 1790s the population of Kentucky tripled, but Methodist membership actually decreased. Fortunately churches and pastors didn't just wring their hands. They folded them in prayer.

The Second Great Awakening began in the early 1800s, but some see its roots in the Northeast in the 1790s. This awakening, too, was a revival that was national in its scope. The main events were camp meetings that sprung up all over the West (today's Midwest) and throughout the frontier. These were outdoor events and/or tent meetings that might draw thousands of people. The one that many historians consider to be the most important was the Cane Ridge Revival in Kentucky that was held August 6-12, 1801. Estimates are that up to 25,000 attended and it became one of the best-reported events in American history. It also ignited this revival movement as it fanned out across the nation. The camp meeting became a staple of American life for the next three decades. Charles Finney was a key player in this period with his revivals in the East. Francis Asbury rode the circuits in the West, traveling an estimated 300,000 miles by horseback or carriage and delivering some 16,500 sermons.

An interesting side-note is that denominational lines were blurred as never before. Many churches worked together to plan and execute these meetings. On the other hand, many new denominations also grew out of this time period.

By the 1830s the Awakening had faded. The growing rift between North and South was leading to The Civil War. Three of the nation's leading denominations all split over slavery or related issues. The division of the Baptists, Methodists and Presbyterians created political fractures that helped to divide the nation.

Slavery is the huge blemish on the face of early American history. (Today's equivalent would be our corporate treatment of the unborn, but that discussion is for another time.) I can't get into all the arguments as to how a "Christian nation" could tolerate and even support slavery, but suffice it to say that the ideals the founders articulated in the Declaration were expected to take time to be fully realized. They knew we couldn't make the changes immediately but trusted that the maturing nation would ultimately develop into one that lived out those ideals.

The Civil War was the most critical time in American history. Not only were the slavery issue being contested, but we were also actually two separate and distinct countries for several years. I hate to think of how we would have fared in the 20ᵗʰ century as two nations instead of one. Just imagine how we would have faced two world wars and the Cold War with all of its issues: the vastness of the Soviet empire, the nuclear arms race and the Cuban missile crisis to name a few if we had never reunited as a nation.

On December 20, 1860, South Carolina became the first state to secede from the union following the election of Abraham Lincoln. Many southern states followed over the next several months to bring the total to eleven that eventually formed the Confederate States of America. The war started in April of 1861 and lasted until April of 1865. In the interim over 620,000 soldiers died—more than all of our other wars combined! And that was with a total North and South population of about 32,000,000 (nearly 4,000,000 of whom were slaves). After the war the southern states gradually rejoined the union over the next five years.

The hidden truth of the Civil War is the revival that immediately preceded the conflict and the conversions that took place during it. In 1858 daily prayer meetings were taking place throughout the country. Called by some the "Third Great Awakening," an estimated 1,000,000 were converted to Christ. During the war between 100,000 and 200,000 soldiers were converted in the Union Army. Among the Confederate troops around 150,000 converted to Christ. At times the Union Army had preaching and praying go on twenty-four hours a day. Often chapels couldn't hold all the soldiers desiring to enter. Millions of tracts were distributed in the North and the South. The U.S. Christian Commission alone put 30,000,000 tracts into soldiers' hands.

We have not seen a revival on a national scale since then. Some believe the last real national revival was actually the Second Great Awakening about 60 years earlier. Many revivals have broken out since, but so have the measles. A spot here and a spot there, but nothing has happened that is national in scope. There has been Dwight Moody, the Azusa Street Revival of 1906, Billy Sunday, Billy Graham, and other leaders and events that have reached many lost people. None have had a truly nationwide impact.

Keep in mind that revival today will likely look different than it looked in previous times. Each one seemed to have its own flavor. Many people remember when God acted mightily in some way and they figure that's what it looks like when God moves. However, God tends to do things in a unique way each time. Check out how many methods Jesus used to heal people—from speaking directly to them to healing long-distance to spitting on the ground and making mud. There was only one world-wide flood with Noah, one Moses and the Red Sea, one David and Goliath, one Elijah taken up by the whirlwind, one Daniel in the lions' den, one conversion of Paul on the road to Damascus, etc. Even where the acts of God were similar, the circumstances were different. The point is, we should anticipate God "doing a new thing." (Isaiah 43:19 NIV) I trust you don't dismiss the hand of God because it does not conform to a tradition that you hold dear. Revival could have all new music, style and culture that have not been seen before as long as it is biblically compatible. The Church has been on the forefront of that many times—especially during the Reformation when new music and culture proliferated. Youth for Christ has had a motto from its early days: "Geared to the times and anchored to the Rock." That ideal could serve any ministry or movement well.

In any case, the only way that a widespread revival is possible is if people pray—and I mean pray like we are desperate. Fervent prayer preceded and was an integral part of all of the revivals we have experienced in our history. In fact, if you study revivals in Scripture, whether in the nation of Israel or among the Apostles, you'll see that prayer was central. The Lord told Moses, "I have indeed seen the misery of my people in Egypt. I have heard them crying out because of their slave drivers, and I am concerned about their suffering." (Exodus 3:7). The Book of Judges records several times that revivals took place after sin became rampant, the people of Israel became oppressed at the hands of a foreign power and they would cry out to God for deliverance. In Acts 1:14, shortly after Jesus had ascended, the twelve disciples (minus Judas Iscariot) "...all joined together <u>constantly in prayer</u>, along with the women and Mary the mother of Jesus, and his brothers." When Pentecost arrived (Acts 2), they were ready to receive what God had for them. The world would forever be changed because of 120 serious pray-ers. Over the centuries revivals have occurred as God's people became serious about seeking Him in the midst of deteriorating cultures. One might think He would tire of this constant cycle, but it seems that our Creator never tires of welcoming backslidden or lost people back into His presence.

Many books are published and many seminars are conducted about prayer. As helpful as they may be, we still need to just PRAY! There doesn't have to be a magic formula. Just go to God and pour it out to Him. Don't worry if it's not profound or eloquent—but it has to be genuine! Be thankful, confess as needed and ask God to pour out His Spirit on our nation. He will hear you.

Significant revivals have happened early in each of the last two centuries. It may just take this kind of movement of God before we genuinely accept our crucial role of funding the Great Commission. Here's to beginning the twenty-first century in such a manner!

Chapter 7

In Their Own Words

—ⅶ—

"Play it again, Sam" was one of the most popular lines never spoken in the movie to which it is attributed. Casablanca is ranked as the best Hollywood movie of all time by some sources. Too bad what many remember is often wrongly quoted. "Money is the root of all evil" is one of the most famous lines never to come out of the Bible. The proper quote is "For the love of money is a root of all kinds of evil." (I Timothy 6:10a NIV) Isn't it amazing what a misplaced word or two can do to mangle the meaning of a statement! "God helps those that help themselves." That sounds biblical and is not an unbiblical principle, but it's not in the Bible.

The rewriting of history can range from misquoting what you thought your mom told you to tell your brother, all the way to fabricating a history of our nation that in no way resembles what actually happened. I checked out a history textbook recently from a local high school that one of my Campus Life students had for homework. In spite of the fact that we have a deep and widespread Christian foundation in the United States, the only references I found that mentioned our spiritual heritage were concerning the Salem witch trials in 1692 and Jonathan Edwards' sermon entitled "Sinners in the Hands of an Angry God." You can, in no way, give any kind of accurate summary of our history by excluding all other religious references. It is not only misleading, it's blatantly false! I would even understand having a negative attitude or a less than favorable opinion toward our founders and their religious tendencies. However, to not even acknowledge the existence of this religious heritage is to rewrite obvious history and is inexcusable.

One issue that really needs to be cleared up is the popular fallacy that the founders were agnostics and deists. A deist believes that God created the earth and turned it loose—that He does not intervene in human affairs. This idea has been propagated through most of our education system for many decades. I don't doubt that deistic ideas were part of the fabric that was woven into the founding of the United States, but they were done so with the overriding tone of orthodox faith.

It's easy to claim what the founders believed if you don't check the facts. The best way to know what someone believes is to discover what they actually said and how they lived. There are about 250 people that are generally considered "founders." They would include the signers of the Declaration of Independence in 1776, the drafters of the Constitution in 1787 and many others such as Patrick Henry, who were very instrumental in our nation's birth. Of these only a very small number would be considered deists. The vast majority were Christians with very biblical beliefs.

Even Ben Franklin was not a deist (although he probably was earlier in his life) at the time the Constitution was developed. Early in the summer of 1787 the constitutional delegates were at a stalemate for several weeks. Franklin addressed the convention: "I have lived, sir, a long time, and the longer I live, the more convincing proof I see of this truth, that God governs the affairs of men. And if a sparrow cannot fall to the ground without His notice, is it probable that an empire can rise without His aid?.......I therefore beg leave to move…that henceforth prayers imploring the assistance of Heaven, and its blessings on our deliberations, be held in the Assembly every morning before we proceed to business, and that one or more of the clergy of this city be requested to officiate in that service." Does that sound like a deist? Asking for "the assistance of Heaven" definitely disqualifies you from Club Deism.

Thomas Jefferson was another famous "deist." Notice how he identifies himself: "I am a real Christian, that is to say, a disciple of the doctrines of Jesus." In all honesty he would not be considered orthodox in his beliefs since he did not believe in the Deity of Jesus. The issue here is what he considered himself to be.

Following are a few of the thousands of quotes by founders that illustrate where they stood regarding their relationship with God:

- "Principally and first of all, I recommend my soul to that Almighty Being who gave it and my body I commit to the dust, relying upon the merits of Jesus Christ for a pardon of all of my sins." **Samuel Adams,** signer of the Declaration of Independence.
- "The religion I have is to love and fear God, believe in Jesus Christ, do all the good to my neighbor, and myself that I can, do as little harm as I can help, and trust on God's mercy for the rest." **Daniel Boone,** Revolutionary officer; Legislator
- "This is the inheritance I can give to my dear family. The religion of Christ can give them one which will make them rich indeed." **Patrick Henry**
- "It cannot be emphasized too clearly and too often that this nation was founded, not by religionists, but by Christians; not on religion, but on the gospel of Jesus Christ. For this very reason, peoples of other faiths have been afforded asylum, prosperity, and freedom of worship here." **Patrick Henry**

- "I believe that there is only one living and true God, existing in three persons, the Father, the Son, and the Holy Ghost, the same in substance equal in power and glory. That the scriptures of the old and new testaments are a revelation from God and a complete rule to direct us how we may glorify and enjoy Him…" **Roger Sherman,** signer of the Declaration of Independence and the Constitution.
- "What students would learn above all in American schools is the religion of Jesus Christ." **George Washington**

George Washington made it quite clear where he stood with regard to his faith, even if he didn't always preach it in public. Following is from his own hand and dated April 21-23, 1752:

"O Most Glorious God, in Jesus Christ, my merciful and loving Father; I acknowledge and confess my guilt in the weak and imperfect performance of the duties of this day. I have called on Thee for pardon and forgiveness of my sins, but so coldly and carelessly that my prayers are become my sin, and they stand in need of pardon."

"I have sinned against heaven and before Thee in thought, word, and deed. I have contemned Thy majesty and holy laws. I have likewise sinned by omitting what I ought to have done and committing what I ought not. I have rebelled against the light, despising Thy mercies and judgment, and broken my vows and promise. I have neglected the better things. My iniquities are multiplied and my sins are very great. I confess them, O Lord, with shame and sorrow, detestation and loathing and desire to be vile in my own eyes as I have rendered myself vile in Thine. I humbly beseech Thee to be merciful to me in the free pardon of my sins for the sake of Thy dear Son and only Savior Jesus Christ who came to call not the righteous, but sinners to repentance. Thou gavest Thy Son to die for me."

A battle cry of the Revolution came from two of our most revered founders, John Adams and John Hancock:

"We Recognize No Sovereign but God, and no King but *Jesus!*" [April 18, 1775]

The other founders include many seminary graduates and those who were members of various Bible societies, missionary societies, etc. For example:

- **John Quincy Adams:** (Sixth President of the United States): Vice-president of the American Bible Society.
- **Alexander Hamilton:** (Signer of the Constitution): Proposed formation of the Christian Constitutional Society to spread Christian government to other nations.
- **John Jay:** (Original Chief Justice of the U.S. Supreme Court): President of the American Bible Society.
- **John Marshall:** (Chief Justice of the U.S. Supreme Court; Secretary of State; Revolutionary General): Vice-President of the American Bible Society; officer in the American Sunday School Union.
- **Benjamin Rush:** (Signer of the Declaration): Founder of the Philadelphia Bible Society.

The list goes on and on. By the evidence that exists (only a tiny fraction of it presented here) none of the founders could be considered to be atheists. A small handful would be what we today call deists. By studying their letters, personal diaries, journals and associations you conclude nothing if not that they were nearly all Bible-believing followers of Christ. Many, if not most, saw a divine purpose unfolding for this new United States.

Chapter 8

Pursuit of the Great Commission

—ᴍ—

How many times have you seen it in the movies—especially westerns or war movies? The hero is seriously injured and as he takes those last few labored breaths, he tells his buddies to make sure that they tell his family or his girl that he loves them.

In Genesis 49, Jacob's last words to his sons were recorded while he and his entire family were still in Egypt. Several of his twelve sons received negative or mixed blessings, some seemed to receive messages that were rather neutral, and a few, notably Judah, were highly blessed. Then he gave strict instructions to bury him back in Canaan along side of Abraham, Sarah, Isaac, Rebekah and his wife Leah. They carried these orders out exactly as stated. Joseph's last words to his people were to make sure that their descendents carry his bones out of Egypt when God brings them into the land He promised. Joseph made them swear it under oath. Four hundred years later, they carried out his order.

Last words are powerful. Think about what you would want people to hear you say just before you left this earth. Most likely you would want to make an impression that would be felt for a long time, and/or you would want to express your love to those closest to you. Either way, you would want to leave a legacy that honors God and stirs those hearing it to remember you fondly or even aspire to a higher level of living.

Jesus delivered the biggest, most important assignment ever given just before He left Planet Earth to stand at the right hand of God (see Acts 7:55-56). The Great Commission has a scope to it that none of us can properly fathom. So huge is this assignment that it appears in Scripture four times as quoted by Jesus (Matthew 28:18-20, Mark 16:15, Luke 24:47-48, Acts 1:8). Imagine the attitude of the twelve disciples when they were told what they would do after He was gone. It had to be totally overwhelming or they just said, "Yeah, right, twelve of us low-income fishermen and such will reach the whole world." Of course, Pentecost came ten days later and within their lifetime the Gospel was taken into much of the known world. The book of Acts mostly records the exploits of Peter and then Paul throughout the Roman Empire, but the rest of the twelve weren't exactly in retirement. For example, Thomas is recognized as taking the Gospel to India in A.D. 52.

The Church experienced periods of prosperity and persecution, times of being outlawed and times of official sanction by the state, times of tremendous growth and times of stagnation. The truth is that God's Great Commission was never in danger of being stopped from the day of Pentecost. When Jesus uttered those words right before His Ascension, He knew that there would ultimately be fulfillment. There were, however, times when it seemed that progress toward this high calling was at a standstill. Throughout history it often looked as if the church would not even survive, let alone grow and prosper.

For example, it looked bleak when the Muslim armies swarmed across much of the Middle East and northern Africa in the 7th and 8th centuries. Many of those areas were

Christian up to that point. Over a dozen centuries later they are still Muslim.

The modern missionary movement began in the late 1700s. Many recognize William Carey from Great Britain as the one who launched it with his voyage to India in 1793. He was not the very first (The first Protestant missionaries arrived in Asia about 100 years earlier), but he is generally recognized as the person who began a huge wave of missionary activity. Great Britain also sent Hudson Taylor to China, David Livingstone to Africa and many others all over the globe. The 19th century was not only the zenith of the British Empire; it was also certainly Great Britain's time for reaching the world for Christ.

In the 20th century the United States assumed the role of world evangelism. Billy Sunday, Youth for Christ, Young Life, Campus Crusade for Christ, Billy Graham, World Vision and many others, not to mention the thousands of missionaries sent by churches and denominations, took the Gospel to most of the people groups in the world. Since my involvement has been in Youth for Christ, I know some of the history of that movement. The actual organization formed in 1944, but its roots were in the many large rallies that were springing up all over the country in the 1930s and 1940s. Each week hundreds, or even thousands, of people would gather in an auditorium or arena to enjoy some entertainment, and hear someone (often a celebrity) give their testimony and present the Gospel. It was the place for Christians to be on a Saturday night. In 1944 many of them gathered in Chicago and organized under the name of Youth for Christ—the name of the program in that city. Torry Johnson, then the director of the Chicago rally, was elected as the first president. His main job was to coordinate events and book speakers for these events. Requests poured in as more and more cities wanted to start their own programs and needed speakers. Torry was still the pastor of a local church and had limited time. Later that year he hired a young Chicago preacher named Billy Graham to travel around the country and speak. He became the first full time YFC staff person. The ministry exploded into a movement that went international the very next year in 1945. Over the next several years many other well-known ministries/organizations found their start via leadership that was coming out of Youth for Christ. World Vision, The Billy Graham Evangelistic Association, Gospel Films, Youth Specialties, Ravi Zacharias International Ministries, and many others have spun off of YFC since its inception.

One particular incident has been carved into my mind even though it happened nine years before I was born. It is memorable because I heard it from the lips of Torry Johnson himself when he spoke to our YFC annual conference in 1991. He was well into his eighties at the time, but still had the fire of passion in his belly that I admire to this day. He spoke of the huge, now legendary rally over Memorial Day weekend in 1945 that took place in Chicago at Soldier Field where the Chicago Bears play football. They had no means to rent the stadium so Torry mortgaged his home in order to do so. The plan was that the offering from the event would cover the expenses. There was some horrendous rain that threatened to turn this into a disaster. They all did some serious praying and with rain all over the Chicago area Soldier Field remained dry. The people showed up 70,000 strong and the event became a powerful witness to God's provision. That kind of faith and risk-taking for the sake of reaching lost people should not be lost on us as we examine how God would have us respond to needs that surround us.

Many other organizations, as mentioned above, have their own stories of heroism, faith and just plain gutsy moves as they played out their God-ordained call. Those kinds of acts continue to this day. They are not limited to "once upon a time." All of us can participate in God's miracles.

Other twentieth century phenomena have been very instrumental in reaching different segments of the population. For example, the Pentecostal/charismatic movement that began in the early 1900's has spread worldwide since then. Thanks to organizations like Wycliffe Bible Translators the Bible was made available in thousands of languages. By 2000 there were very few people who didn't have some kind of access to the message of Christ. Today most of the denied access is because of political, not linguistic reasons.

In addition, over the last decade or so of the 20ᵗʰ century a major shift was taking place. The main stage for church growth was moving from the western world to Africa and Asia. The numbers are staggering and unprecedented. Many thousands come to Christ each day in the non-western world. Not only that, but now they're sending missionaries to us! That is the reason we must retool our view of the role we play as American Christians in this new century.

Chapter 9

What Makes the 21st Century so Crucial?

—∿∿—

For the last 500 years the pace of life and world events seems to have been accelerating more with every passing century. (I realize that I'm speaking primarily from a Western Civilization point of view. Admittedly I am not nearly as familiar with the history of Africa and Asia—especially as pertaining to pre-20th century history.) The Renaissance, the Reformation, the invention of the printing press and the beginning of world exploration all started and/or developed momentum around the 15th and 16th centuries. Before that there was your typical rise and fall of kingdoms, a few inventions made the scene and some key people made their mark on the world. Starting around 1500 the world would change significantly as each 100-year milestone was marked:

1500s: World exploration is cranked up primarily by Spain but also several other nations. The Reformation kicks into high gear and transforms much of Europe.

1600s: Colonization of the New World (Western Hemisphere)

1700s: American and French Revolutions have a huge impact and pave the way for change in the way nations are governed. (Although there is a monster difference in the causes and effects of these two revolutions, they did both initiate major changes.)

1800s: The Industrial Revolution promoted a change from agrarian to industrial-based societies. Machines began to do much of the work formerly done by human or animal power. Inventions proliferated. By now much of the world had been colonized by European nations.

1900s: With two world wars, the Cold War, the rise and fall of Communism (primarily in the Soviet Union), we transitioned into the Information Age from the Industrial Age, the Nuclear Age was ushered in, and the Internet transformed how we do business.

What do we have to anticipate for the 21ˢᵗ century? First, let's take a look at the general lay of the land:

- We entered the new century with over six billion people inhabiting the planet. In 1900 the world population was about 1.6 billion. What might we be looking at in 2100?
- It seems that radical Islam will be to this century what Communism was to the last one. We are probably in this for the long haul.
- In numerous ways the environment has improved in the 20ᵗʰ century. Many areas stripped of their trees for wood and fuel have been reforested. Rivers have been cleaned up and are once again good recreation areas. But that is not true around the world. Clean water is increasingly a challenge and other major environmental issues will have to be addressed as

the developing world industrializes with a growing population.

- The youth culture is more and more becoming a battleground between the spiritual and secular worlds. Some experts feel that the media has a larger influence on the next generation than the church. Most indicators seem to point in that direction. Parents are finding it necessary to monitor, not just friends and substance abuse, but also media consumption and the Internet. Anticipating the next generation's leadership in our culture gives many people cause for great concern.

- Atheism and secularism will increasingly battle traditional Christian values and culture. Many believe that Europe is already lost to secularism. Church attendance over there ranges from about two percent in France to a high of ten percent in England. One of the highest values of a secular culture is tolerance. That basically means anything goes as long as you don't hurt anybody. It sounds reasonable on the surface but the tolerance is often ABC (Anything But Christ). In our country Christian roots go deep, as we saw in previous chapters. Over time there has been more tolerance for those who could hold leadership positions. Early on in our history as colonies, you had to be a believer in Christ from a certain denomination to be elected to public office. Later on you could be from any Protestant church. Then you had to be at least from a Christian background, and later on at least be monotheistic. Eventually it was okay just as long as you're not an Atheist. By the middle of the 20ᵗʰ century anybody could be elected to or appointed to a governing role. The secularists were finally "in the boat." They soon decided that the boat was too crowded and started to kick the Christians out. Many decisions by the courts have totally ignored the Constitution. Separation of church and state has been the rallying cry for decades. That concept is <u>not</u> in the Constitution. It all comes from a letter that Thomas Jefferson wrote to the Danbury Baptists in Connecticut in 1802. They were concerned about the possibility of an official state church and wrote him to address that concern. In his reply he speaks of a "wall of separation" but he goes on to explain that the whole idea was to keep the government away from meddling in the church, not vice versa. There is plenty of good writing on this issue so I won't pursue it here. Suffice it to say that we have seen thousands of court rulings that invoke this principle that first, is <u>not even in our founding documents</u>, and second, is <u>misused time and time again from what Thomas Jefferson's letter stated</u>.

In light of all of this, can we make it through the 21ˢᵗ century reasonably intact? When you consider that Communist leaders (all were officially atheistic) were responsible for the deaths of about 100,000,000 people in the 20ᵗʰ century, you can only wonder what we're in for at the hands of terrorists in this century. Under terrorism the numbers are not that huge so far, but it's the other unknowns that make it unsettling. There is not a country that can be attacked or even negotiated with to counter terrorist acts. They believe they are doing God's will. You can't negotiate with that.

The other unsettling aspect comes when you realize that more Christians were killed for their belief in Jesus in the twentieth century than in the previous nineteen combined. What could be in store for the church as we progress through this time?

All of these issues make the case for some believers that the Second Coming of Jesus is imminent. It may be imminent, but that doesn't mean it's immediate. There have been for many centuries, times and circumstances that led Christians to think He was returning now. Many despots were thought to be the Anti-Christ over the last two millennia. Persecution would feed the flame of watching for His return. Some even set dates. So far all of the dates have passed. They must have skipped the verse where Jesus says that nobody knows the day except the Father (Matthew 24:36). When I was fifteen I heard a speaker talk about the Second Coming in June and I felt certain that I would never be around for the start of football camp two months later on August 18. I read books that practically guaranteed He would return in a few years at the most. Decades later: I still believe it could all happen in my lifetime. Some world situations make it look like it must be soon. If the truth would be known, Israel could get pushed back into the Mediterranean Sea for a couple hundred more years. We could see major breakthroughs in food production, and other technologies to take care of what many now think will be impossible-to-support numbers of people on the planet. There may be colonization of space. The point is we don't know when Christ returns. What we do know is that we need to be about the business He has called us to: Reaching a lost and hurting world.

To me all of these issues make the pursuit of the Great Commission that much more critical. We can't waste time on petty things like chasing a lifestyle or circling the wagons just to hunker down and hope it goes away. The main thing we cannot do is put energy into fighting each other. I have pictured the Enemy laughing hysterically over Christians getting into petty squabbles about fine points of doctrine, personalities, ego-trips and on and on. We suck all the oxygen out of the room by fighting each other. How many denominations are only making news because of their annual wrangling about gay marriage or ordination at their conventions? What energy is then left to address the Great Commission? And we wonder why those institutions have been losing members for decades? The Enemy wins a great victory when we spend our resources on distractions. Hey, eternity lasts a long time. Let's invest ourselves in that.

There are a couple of realities that may seem to be negative on the surface, but a closer look will offer encouragement. For one thing, denominational loyalty is fast becoming a thing of the past. A generation or so ago when a Presbyterian family moved into town, they would find and attend the Presbyterian Church—their particular brand of Presbyterian Church. That is much less the case today.

Secondly, there is more of a consumer mentality and people will shop around for a church that meets their needs regarding programming, preaching style, friendliness, etc. A particular doctrine that a denomination would historically hold does not factor into the decision as much as in the past. In fact, a large Presbyterian church in our area just called a senior pastor who is a Methodist! If you know the significant differences in their respective beliefs, that could come as a shock. They have literally opposite positions in certain doctrines. Obviously people, and even pulpit committees are not seeing those as issues. I admit there's a downside to doctrinal ignorance, but the good news to this is that it creates a little competition and forces churches to be more diligent about growth and what they offer to the public. They can't assume that everyone from their denomination will show up. That helps to explain the proliferation of large non-denominational mega-churches. Most of these are independent (or their affiliation is very low-keyed); they have great programming and people with a wide variety of church backgrounds. The doctrine (at least what is preached regularly) is quite basic and would find agreement among most believers. The main issue is not so much doctrinal purity as it is living a

Christ-like life in order to reach out to others. I applaud these churches since they are reaching an audience that a traditional church couldn't touch. I guess my history of valuing evangelism as part of YFC explains my views—anything the Church can do to reach the lost is a good thing.

A great example of this is the Hot Metal Bridge Church in Pittsburgh's South Side. My oldest son is active there and it is anything but a "traditional church." Full of Gen-X-ers with tattoos and piercings, Hot Metal is reaching a whole population of people that few other churches are even aware of, much less reach out to them. Maybe the best story here is that this church was planted as a joint venture of the Pittsburgh Presbytery and the Western PA Conference of the United Methodist Church. One of the pastors is a Presbyterian; the other is a Methodist. I know some of you are shaking your heads since, as mentioned above; these two denominations have some areas of theology in which they actually contradict each other. Well, that doesn't matter a bit to 99% of the several hundred who attend. The leadership understands that the main issue is to reach lost people—most of whom need to know Jesus and don't give a hoot for that level of theological detail.

The fact is that there is more unity in the general Body of Christ than there has been in generations. Churches are working together more than ever to impact their communities. We have gotten past the "enclave" mentality and are engaging the world better today than at any time in most of our memories. That is a positive by-product of blurring denominational lines. I absolutely believe that if the churches in a given community bonded together in any effort, they would be unstoppable. Picture all the churches in your town claiming "we are going to reach that high school for Christ" or "let's clean up this drug-infested area." Who could or would want to stop that? The 21ˢᵗ century will be an unprecedented time of outreach because of the increasing unity in the Body of Christ.

There is no choice. We must aggressively pursue the Great Commission with every resource available. With Jesus as the Head of the church we are assured of adequate resources and wisdom. The question remains: Will we tap into what He offers or decide on another route? As you have seen, I don't think we are the world's richest country because of our unparalleled virtues. For some reason God has raised up this incredibly prosperous nation to fit into His plan. Let us make our mark on this century, as we become a conduit of His blessings to the rest of the world.

Chapter 10

Our Role in
The Great Commission

—◊◊◊—

The United States is no longer the center of gravity with regard to church growth or missionary activity in the world. Nonetheless, the biggest assignment ever given to the church was the Great Commission. It is articulated in some form by Jesus four times in the New Testament—Matthew, Mark, Luke and Acts. If God has formed this nation, then there is a part we are designed to play in the Great Commission.

So just what is our role as American Christians in the 21st Century? Again, our unique role in the 21st century is to <u>fund the Great Commission</u>. We are the only ones capable of fulfilling this job description.

There are two elements necessary to fulfill this massive vision:

1. **The ability:** (The necessary economic engine.)
2. **The desire:** (A mission-minded, generous population.)

Ours is the only nation on the planet with an adequate amount of both of these elements available. As far as ability goes, Billy Graham once claimed that there is enough money in American bank accounts to fulfill the Great Commission. (That statement planted one of the first seeds in my mind that led to this book.) The amazing part of this is that it could be done without a serious crimp in our lifestyles—that's how prosperous this nation is. I found one source that claims Americans have over ten billion dollars just lying around as loose change. There are many nations that don't even have economies of that size. Giving ten percent would not drive us into poverty. I recognize that ten percent is not the legal standard in the New Testament, but it is the standard in much of the Old Testament.

The main New Testament message is to give according to how God has blessed you and out of the abundance of your heart. "On the first day of the week, each one of you should set a side a sum of money in keeping with his income…" (I Corinthians 16:2 NIV) I think Paul sums it up quite well in his first letter to Timothy: "Command those who are rich in this present world not to be arrogant nor to put their hope in wealth, which is so uncertain, but to put their hope in God, who richly provides us with everything for our enjoyment. Command them to do good, to be rich in good deeds, and to be generous and willing to share. In this way they will lay up treasure for themselves as a firm foundation for the coming age, so that they may take hold of the life that is truly life." (I Timothy 6:17-19 NIV) If you take into consideration the wealth of this nation, ten percent could well be just a starting point—and I'm just talking about regular income at this point. Additionally, other levels of stewardship could be addressed with regard to assets and estate planning. More will be said about that in the next chapter.

The main issue might be whether we actually have the desire to give generously to further God's work by funding the Great Commission. The ability is obvious. Often the heart only follows when some intense experience drives it that way. Many foundations and large gifts to charity are the result of losing a loved one to illness or disease. Frequently whole communities will hold fund-raising events to pay for surgery or treatment of an ill person when they don't have the ability to pay or adequate insurance. People will also band together to provide a college fund for children who have lost a bread-winning parent. How many millions were raised for the families of 9-11 victims? It all comes down to a condition of the heart. I trust that God will motivate our population to generosity. A fund-raising seminar I once attended put it well: "There is no scarcity of money, just a lack of well-articulated causes."

Regarding the Great Commission on a personal level we have two choices—we can either go or we can send. Actually we need to do both. Going may sound too adventurous for some of us, but in reality we can all go in some form. Going does not have to mean slogging it out with the Aborigines in New Guinea with 100-degree heat and no running water. (Thank God there are those called to reach people in that situation.) Going might mean going next door and being kind to your neighbor. It might mean looking for a need that someone has and meeting that need. A Christian should never be bored. The mission field is all around us.

At the same time you might have the means and desire to send missionaries. Even if you don't have a great deal of money to support God's work you can pray for them. I know many people who are prayer warriors—doing battle on their knees. That is not just a cute, trite little slogan. It is an actual description of what goes on when you are in prayer. That is where you confront the forces of darkness and bring the name of Jesus to bear in genuine battle. Check out Ephesians 6:10-18 (the armor of God passage) or the time when Jesus confronted the evil spirit in a boy (Mark 9:14-29). The disciples could not drive it out but Jesus did. They asked why they couldn't and Jesus replied, "This kind can come out only by prayer." Prayer IS the battle!

Another way we can send missionaries is to make sure that the next generation has a relationship with and a desire to serve Jesus. In the last chapter I raised a concern about today's youth. There are some indicators that cause alarm, but there are also many reasons to find hope for our future as a nation and in the world. On top of that, there had better be hope. As a Bible teacher on the radio once stated, "We are always just twenty years away from barbarism." In other words, if one generation is ever cut off from the gospel, we will not only lose that generation, but we will inaugurate a culture of barbarism. That creates an urgency to reach the next generation. Funding youth ministry is always a good investment.

What gives me hope for our future is that millions of American teenagers want something radically different than the moral bankruptcy produced by us baby-boomers. We are experiencing the hangover from a sexual revolution that many teens are not only paying for, but are rejecting, as well. Don't get me wrong—kids are still kids. They are discovering the world, pushing limits and taking chances. However, teen rebellion used to be sneaking away to drink, do drugs or experiment sexually. Now many Christian teenagers are rebelling by praying in school, starting a Christian club, going on mission trips overseas, or sharing Christ with a friend. As adults we must support our children in the face of what is being thrown at them. Up until about the mid-1960s, parents could turn their children loose on the culture for the most part. Television, schools and other aspects of our society generally reinforced what was taught at home. That is no longer the case. If a child is not involved in church or some other ministry, they can go through the entire day and not see any indication of God, or especially, of any Christian relevance in the world. Parents today must be deliberate and intentional in passing their values to their children. The default setting is receiving their values from TV, movies and other media sources. "Fix these words of mine in your hearts and minds...Teach them to your children, talking about them when you sit at home and when you walk along the road, when you lie down and when you get up." (Deuteronomy 11:18-19 NIV) No matter what the culture throws at us, God promises that His word will be effective. Our job is to make sure that the next generation has a chance to hear it.

This can be a time that accelerates the fulfillment of the Great Commission even faster than the pace that has been happening over the past couple of decades. Because of the wealth of missionary activity that has occurred over the last 200 years, there is a church structure in place around the world that is being turned loose. We no longer need to send as many of our people there to reach the lost. In fact, they are doing their own evangelism with their own people in a powerful way — without cultural or language barriers. Often the role of our missionaries is to train leaders, teach in seminaries and equip the local evangelists in numerous ways. We also send doctors, construction crews, and other support services while indigenous Christians present the Gospel to their own people.

Therefore, we must support the work of those who spread the Gospel in every nation. We can pay for several full time indigenous workers for the cost of sending just one of our own missionaries. That does not eliminate the need for us to go. It simply means that our role is changing and we need to invest in those who can best reach their own people.

Regarding your personal role in this huge task, learn to be creative when it comes to how you can serve God and contribute to the Great Commission. You can give of your time and your talent as well as your treasure. No matter what you have or what you can do, there is a way to parlay that into changing lives.

Chapter 11

What if?

—〰—

He was an All-State football player and had just returned from winning the state basketball championship, forcing a late start in track season. I'm not sure he had even been to a practice yet, but there he was marking off his steps for the long jump. I watched him stutter-step his way down the runway, not reaching anywhere near full speed, and launch himself into the air with a leap that would make any kangaroo jealous. This guy jumped twenty-two feet with that miserable looking approach! (My best in high school was 20½ feet—a school record at the time.) It was a performance that could let anybody compete at the state level. I can only imagine how he jumped with a little more practice.

Football scholarship offers were numerous—he could have written his own ticket. This guy had athletic ability that is seen in few people. It's likely he had the physical tools to go into professional ball right out of high school. That's unheard of in football. He started his freshman year at a division 1-A school and had his bumps, but they didn't seem to be insurmountable. Soon he encountered academic trouble, some other issues arose and eventually he seemed to be in a total meltdown. I don't know all the details, but he never played much football after that. The newspapers all speculated what might have been.

"What if?" can be a painful question. The unrealized potential of a person or a team or an organization, especially when there's an absurd amount of talent, seems like such a waste. God has equipped that person or team or organization for a certain role. I don't want to be the one who faces the Lord and says "...I knew that you are a hard man...so I was afraid and went out and hid your talent in the ground." (Matthew 25:24-25 NIV)

"What if?" can also be a hopeful question. As you read the following paragraphs, let's look at the hope that we are capable of spreading to a hurting and lost world.

There is some good news and some not-as-good news regarding this hope:

- The good news is that we are already the most generous nation in the world and by far support more of God's work than anyone.
- The not-as-good news is that we give away less of our wealth by percentage than most of our poorer Christian brethren around the world. We also give less now as a percentage of income than we did in the Great Depression. The only reason it's not "bad news" is that what we are doing is good—it just could be so much better.

The Barna Update (April 25, 2005) indicated that just 6% of Americans tithed (donated at least 10% of their income to a church or non-profit organization) in 2004. That number was 27% among evangelical Christians. That could be somewhat encouraging until you also realize that less than 2% of adults under the age of 40 are tithing. The reasons Americans do not give more as interpreted by Barna:

- "...the church has failed to provide a compelling vision for how the money will make a difference in the world."
- "...they do not see a sufficient return on their investment."
- "...do not realize the church needs their money to be effective."
- "...ignorant of what the Bible teaches about our responsibility to apply God's resources in ways that affect lives."
- "...those who are just selfish.....Priorities revolve around their personal needs and desires."

If American Christians can overcome these barriers, we will see unprecedented numbers of people won to Christ. We will also see an incredible amount of suffering all over the world eased or even eliminated.

However, it's not just about scattering dollars across our country and around the world. We also have a long way to go in funding those that God has called into ministry. There is a "warrior class" that attacks ministry in much the same way that the warrior class of soldier attacks the enemy—with incredible zeal and energy. These people must do what God has called and equipped them to do or they feel like they'll explode. I know well the feeling. I was that warrior class. As soon as I graduated college, I went to work building the Youth for Christ/Campus Life ministry in the two school districts to which I was assigned. The energy and passion I put into that mission still makes my head spin when I think about it. I went 70 to 80 hours per week without any second thought. I ate, drank, slept and breathed Campus Life for seven years. What did it matter—I was single. There was no hesitation to go the second mile...or the third...or the fourth. I had to reach every kid in those schools with the gospel! I took one week of vacation in five years. That's not taking my "martyr pills." I loved doing the work. It was a joy to such a degree that I had a hard time believing that this was my "job" and I was getting paid to do this. The Apostle Paul said, "...I am compelled to preach. Woe to me if I do not preach the gospel!" (I Corinthians 9:16 NIV)

There are untold thousands of these warriors that would love to report for duty. I can't tell you how many people I personally know who would love to get into ministry, but their main barrier is financial. They feel they can't make enough money to survive in ministry and/or they have a real anxiety about fund raising. The above issues must be addressed and it must be done without driving the guilt machine regarding potential donors. A "compelling vision" alone (as mentioned above by Barna) will go a long way toward funding the Great Commission.

The above information can either create despair ("We're not doing enough.") or hope ("Look at the incredible potential we have!"). I choose the latter and believe God is preparing us to do the job He designed for us. When you look at the massive amount of wealth that our economy generates and see what could be done regarding the Great Commission, it's very encouraging. Our economy has been doubling about every ten years. The Gross Domestic Product (GDP) is the total of all goods and services produced by our nation. The GDP has increased by approximately 100% each decade since the 1950s. Today our economy is producing nearly $14,000,000,000,000 (that's trillion!) worth of activity in a year. Less than two percent of that amount goes to charitable causes. It's true that $260,000,000,000 (that's billion) is a lot of money given by private donors to charity in a year. Individuals give the vast majority of those funds (83.2%) to charity. Foundations (11.5%) and corporations (5.3%) make up the balance of charitable giving. (Forty percent of that $260 billion is given to churches.) Just imagine what would be possible if that "compelling vision" gripped more of the nation.

Here is a challenge: Consider "1% a year up to 10%." Increase your giving by one percent of your income per year until it reaches ten percent. In ten years we would all be at least at a tithe level. Can you imagine what could be done if that kind of money were turned loose to build God's kingdom? When you consider that most American Christians give less than five per cent to charitable causes, that could mean many billions of additional dollars to reach the lost, feed the hungry, dig wells, provide housing, meet medical needs and do many other things that are severely needed around the globe. Here's another challenge: Is that percentage before or after taxes are taken out of the paycheck? That's one of the issues with which you must wrestle.

Altogether there are three pockets from which we can draw in order to finance the Great Commission.

- The first pocket (mentioned above) is giving out of your income.
- The second pocket is giving of your assets. Donations of real estate, appreciated stock or other assets can give you great tax benefits and also provide significant support for ministry. If any asset has appreciated in value, you can donate it and the funds go to the ministry instead of being taxed by the government.
- The third pocket is estate planning. Who or what will benefit from the wealth God has entrusted to you upon your passing? There are ways to set up your estate so that you can give generously to your church or other ministry, saving that money from being taxed by the government and still provide all you want to go to your heirs.

What if millions of American Christians began to see their fortune of being born in this nation as more than luck or even just God's blessing for them? <u>What if</u> millions of American Christians began to see that even U.S. citizens of modest means are rich compared to most of the world? <u>What if</u> millions of American Christians realized that God created this gold mine of wealth for His purposes? <u>What if</u> millions of Americans rolled up their sleeves and said, "It's time to make this happen?"

What if all believers in our nation gave ten percent of their time and used their talent to change lives around them? Here are some options:

- Millions of lonely people in assisted living, hospitals and prison would receive visits from many who have gifts of listening, conversation and encouragement. Some of this requires training, but much of it just requires time and a willingness to listen.
- Find a ministry that does something that is close to your heart and volunteer your talent. Homeless shelters (Salvation Army, etc.), youth ministries (Young Life, Youth for Christ, Fellowship of Christian Athletes, etc.), relief agencies (World Vision, Samaritan's Purse, Compassion International, etc.), building low-income housing (Habitat for Humanity, etc.), and other organizations are available to provide an outlet to express your gift.
- Walk around your neighborhood and pray for God to give you opportunities to serve and share Christ. Treat it like God has called you to that "parish."
- Churches always need people to be involved. The 80/20 principle is usually the norm. Eighty percent of the work is done by twenty percent of the people. The leadership of the church would be thrilled to have you involved.
- Pray. I know many who are not able to be very active in ministry due to health or mobility issues, but they have a connection with the living God that is to be

envied. They often yield incredible results. I think God wants all of us to be effective prayer warriors. If you need to build a more solid relationship with your Creator, do what it takes to make that happen. Then your prayers will do way more than seemingly bounce off of the ceiling. "The prayer of a righteous man is powerful and effective." (James 5:16b NIV) That is the only hope we have for national revival.

- Find ways that children, even young children, can serve. If they are brought up reaching out to others, it will be a pattern that will stay with them for life. Most of the items listed are appropriate for teenagers. Of course, always know well the situation you are entering and never compromise safety. Younger children should be involved by going along side of adults at first to observe and then gradually participating in well-supervised service.

Some of you are scanning all of those activities and not seeing anything that lights you up. Maybe you like to work on cars, or you love to hit the slopes on a snowboard, or you're into needlepoint. No matter what you like to do, where you like to go, or what you collect, you can use your passion to touch other lives. You can do it with people, bring young people along side of you, or teach it. It does not have to be blatantly "spiritual" to serve God. Even studying the feeding habits of dung beetles qualifies. "So whether you eat or drink or whatever you do, do it all for the glory of God." (I Corinthians 10:31 NIV) We can honor God in whatever we do.

In Malachi, the last book of the Old Testament, God put out a powerful challenge. After accusing the people of robbing Him by not bringing in the whole tithe, God said, "Test me in this, and see if I will not throw open the floodgates of heaven and pour out so much blessing that you will not have room enough for it." (Malachi 3:10 NIV)

We live in the richest, most prosperous nation in all of history. God has given Americans stewardship of this immense wealth. About the last thing I want to be is one who robs God. We answer to Him regarding that steward-ship—whether it's the stewardship of time, talent or trea-sure. We can also turn this thing around. Let's see this 21ˢᵗ century as our opportunity to impact the world in a way that will resound for billions of years in eternity.

Chapter 12

Getting Past Our Money Hang-ups

—⁊⁊⁊—

Now it gets personal. Reading this material is fine since it generically addresses the entire nation. No one has to feel like it's aimed directly at him or her. As a result it's still "safe" to read. Well, maybe it IS aimed at you.

I have seen countless times, two opposite extremes in how people respond to money—more specifically, how Christians respond:

First, "Money is not that important," or even "Christians shouldn't have a lot of money." This has been a mantra among too many believers. Nowhere is this truer than with those in vocational ministry. My three decades in Youth for Christ have shown me that a large number of people in ministry have a poverty mentality. I'm not just picking on YFC. My exposure to other organizations and churches proves this to be very universal among those who are paid to do ministry. I know we must be good stewards of the resources entrusted to us and we cannot plan on making a huge salary from those who donate of their treasure. The issue is that (and I have fallen for this myself) some feel that we are "called" to a life of relative poverty. I have gotten into discussions with other ministers where we all bragged about how many miles were on our cars or how little we spent on certain items. I believe there are very few that God has "called" into poverty. We live in the most prosperous nation in history. That does not warrant an apology or guilt.

The other factor in this extreme is the expectation that those in ministry should exist at a subsistence level. I've heard too many instances when a donor will make a judgment call on a purchase that was made by someone in full time ministry. The implication is "look how they're spending my money." That should never be an issue. That money is given to the Lord way before it's given to the organization or person. The donor's act of stewardship is giving to the ministry. After that the stewardship of those dollars is between the organization or employee and God. Believe me, I am always sensitive to the fact that donors have made it possible for me to conduct ministry. Therefore, I try to be the steward of those resources that I should be, but my first loyalty in that department is to the Lord. At times I have even questioned how dollars that I have donated have been used. But it's not my responsibility to judge how an individual allocates those funds when he/she makes family decisions.

There's one incident where a staff prospect was being interviewed for a position with an organization and was asked, "What's the minimum you can live on? That's what we'll pay you." It was hard to wrap my mind around that one. The organization should say, "We will pay you as well as possible so you can live reasonably within the community in which you minister." Too often spouses are forced to work even with young children at home when the family would rather be able to make it on one income.

I experienced for myself the judgment of a donor who became a former donor after seeing what I paid for my house by viewing the listing of deeds filed in the newspaper. He basically said that if I can afford that house, I didn't need his money. The house was 80 years old, but was in the community in which I did ministry—I thought it best to live in that area. The house was priced below the median for the area and I knew for a fact that his household income was at least double mine. It bothered me for a while, but that's between he and the Lord.

Hey, there is nothing wrong with "tent-making" or having a supplemental income to improve your situation. I also don't believe there's such a thing as too much money! If we believers don't control God's wealth, who will? Those resources are just what God can use to advance His agenda. We should be in the middle of that!

Second, the "name-it-and-claim-it" gospel is not what Jesus had in mind either. He did not place this unprecedented level of wealth before us just to bless us. We are to be a conduit of that blessing. The richest people I know are just those types of conduits. They love to bless others and God keeps blessing them. That's the kind of upward spiral you want in your life! The blessings I'm referring to aren't all material. Much of this comes in the form of time and energy and relationships as well. Some very wealthy people are also very miserable. If they would bless others, they just might experience unspeakable joy.

A few years ago my wife and I attended a conference and heard a speaker talk about how families tend to operate in this prosperous culture. He stated that too many American homes have become centers of consumption instead of centers of production. That really stuck with me! I have meditated on that simple statement countless times since and have become determined that our home would be much less of the former and much more of the latter. I'm sure we have failed in that ideal multiple times but I know that just keeping that concept in mind has had a positive effect and has probably prevented many poor decisions.

People in all situations can have hang-ups about money. Rich and poor can have bad attitudes and a poverty mentality. They both can think that more money will solve their problems. That is likely not the issue. The root of all of this is spiritual. That's why many others, rich and poor, have a great attitude, are generous and love life. They have settled the issue of who owns it all. There is great freedom in owning nothing but allowing God to bless as He chooses and enjoying those blessings as we manage what He has entrusted to us. That is how we could finance the Great Commission and do it joyfully.

My job is not to judge what car anyone should drive, what kind of home they should live in or what kind of vacations they should take. My goal is to awaken people to the issue of stewardship regarding the resources God has entrusted to their care. I do know this much—there is incredible joy in giving—whether it be of your treasure, your time or your talent. God wants to bless you abundantly but that doesn't mean we are all supposed to be rich in the financial sense. Our culture is replete with stories of those who came into a lot of money, either through inheritance, the lottery, or some other means where they did not work for it. More often than not their lives were in chaos before a year or two had expired. If we follow Christ, He will not allow us to have what we cannot handle. It could be that God has and/or will prosper you with some talent, in relationships, or in the ability to love people and touch their lives. Whatever it is that God has gifted to you, use it to honor Him and change lives forever. In Israel the Dead Sea is dead because it only has an intake for the waters of the Jordan River. There is no outlet. The Sea of Galilee is teaming with life because it receives and gives—it's a conduit of the Jordan's riches.

There is no question that money is an important issue. Jesus spoke about it more than any other topic. Among many references to money in the Scriptures, He stated, "For where your treasure is, there your heart will be also." (Luke 12:34 NIV) Notice Jesus said that our heart follows the money, not the other way around. Put your money in the right direction and your heart will go there. That likely means that you'll pray and give of yourself in that direction: maybe some of your time and talent as well as funds. Letting the money follow your heart might not lead you in the right way.

The overall message here is: Live Abundant and Be Generous. Living in the richest country in all of history is a reality. Get over it! Above all, know that God has placed you and I in this national wealth machine for a reason. Let's find that reason and let's get busy blessing others.

Chapter 13

What Will Be Your Wake-up Call?

—⚍—

Two friends of ours had serious health issues. Both had wake-up calls. Both had very different results. Gregg* would always complain about shortness of breath, fatigue and other symptoms. Our ongoing counsel to him was to see a doctor but our efforts were ignored. We knew he was a ticking time bomb. One day as he sat down on his front stoop to take a break while cutting grass, the bomb detonated. He died almost instantly from a massive heart attack. Doug* was at his funeral and knew what he had to do in light of the symptoms he was experiencing as well. After a visit to the doctor Doug very soon had multiple by-pass heart surgery.

Same wake-up call. Vastly different results.

Back in chapter two I explained how God used a time when I lay in a hospital bed having just lost all of the things around which I had built my life. What I interpreted as a life in ruins was really a wake-up call that God was using to redirect my passion and energy.

When an issue is of prime importance to God, He will make sure we get the message. We can stick our head in the sand, run away, distract ourselves with other activities or try to ignore Him. His ways are subtle but they are inevitable. You will eventually come around to that. But the warning is: The longer and more stubbornly you hold out, the more miserable you will become. God won't necessarily scream at you through a cosmic PA system or fire bolts of lightning, but He will, without tiring, keep bringing you back around to face where you need to be until you decide to go with His plan. At the time of your conversion, He took you at your word when you said you were giving your life to Him. That gave Him the right to "meddle." He only meddles in the lives of those that belong to Him. We gave Him permission to do so.

Now that sounds like a raw deal upon further examination—especially when He meddles with certain areas. The key here is that He is a loving father. He provides the greatest of gifts—including His Son. No coal in this Christmas stocking!

So just what will it take for you to really say, "God, it's all yours. I make no more claims on anything. You own it all." Possibly this message triggers a wake-up call in a totally different category than stewardship of funds. No matter what, it is still a stewardship issue regarding your time, talent, or anything that God has entrusted to you. Or what will it take for you to make the next move of obedience that you know is required? Will it take a severe wake-up call? A significant amount of pain could be avoided if you act sooner than later.

*Names changed

96

Chapter 14

Find Your Passion

—〰—

D o you remember why the Dead Sea is dead? Right, it takes in but doesn't give out. God has designed us to be at our best when we give ourselves away. The happiest, most fulfilled people I know are those who are generous with their time, their talent and their treasure. The most miserable people I know are those that hoard whatever they can of those resources.

Your next thought might be, "What do I have that I can contribute? What do I have that anybody could need or want? I don't have a lot of money and have just average talent."

There are times when you have to dig deep. Let me tell you what average does:

- Average people walked <u>into</u> the burning World Trade Center buildings on 9-11 and saved thousands of lives. Many gave theirs in the process.
- An average church member gave several thousand dollars to help begin a Youth for Christ chapter in 1985 that today thrives and reaches thousands of lost teenagers with the gospel of Christ.
- An average teenager has undertaken his own abolitionist movement by starting something called Loose

Change for Loose Chains to help free slaves around the world. (See www.myspace.com/lc2lc)
- Every day average people are sharing Christ with family, friends, neighbors and co-workers. As a result, they are having an impact on eternity.

Why can't <u>we</u> be involved in doing spectacular things? Why can't we expect God to get us in on that action? Why will heroic deeds always be performed by someone else or only be seen in the movies? WHY NOT US?! Look at what Paul tells the Ephesians: "Now to him who is able to do immeasurably more than all we ask or imagine, according to his power that is at work within us..." (Ephesians 3:20 NIV) Notice the last word in that passage—us. That's you and me. **We all have the God-given right to expect that our lives will be immeasurably more than we can ask or even imagine!** God designed us to be involved in something bigger than ourselves. We do not need to be living "little lives." No matter how old you are and how awesome your past, your best days could still be in front of you. By the same token, no matter how many regrets or how checkered your past, the same grace is for you. His grace is bigger than any skeleton in your closet.

Please understand that this is not just a pep talk to get you psyched for a while. That's great for football games, but that level of intensity cannot be maintained for long without smoke coming out of your ears. It is also not just hype so that you can just feel good for a little while. It is a biblical fact that you were created for greatness. Notice I didn't say fame or riches. Greatness in the eyes of God means significance and the capacity to change lives forever. That is simply a fact. It may not be flashy or get you on Oprah, but it will give you a deep level of satisfaction and purpose.

How does that play itself out on a day-to-day basis? <u>First, you need to discover your passion</u>. You may know this already and now simply must decide to pursue it. Possibly, you just feel numb because life beat you up and you are bleeding. No matter what your condition, inside of you lies the powerhouse of some kind of passion. You may not even recognize it, but it's there. Do whatever you need to do to find it. Get counseling, life-coaching, talk with trusted family and friends and have people pray for you. I had to go through all of those routes to find mine. It was a search that felt desperate at times, resulted in a few dead ends, and took a few years, but it was worth every tear, anxiety attack and feeling of worthlessness.

Maybe you are thinking, "What does my passion look like and how will I know if I found it?" The thing I am certain of is that it is in there. God has planted passion in the heart of every person. <u>Your job</u> is to dig for it. For openers, think about those things that bring tears to your eyes that go beyond superficial emotion. Is there a certain type of movie or type of story that moves you on a deep level? Are you exposed to situations that do the same—situations that involve pain, hunger, injustice, poverty, children's issues, education or cultural and moral issues? I finally figured out that situations that involve overcoming huge odds or making the impossible comeback move me at a very deep level. Guess what. American history is loaded with those scenarios. It was a great match since I have such a love for our nation's Christian heritage. Don't expect this process to be completed in an hour or two—especially if you are muddling through some intense personal issues. After you discover your passion you still have to figure out how to translate that into a way that will touch the lives of those God puts in your path. It could even be career related, but it may be strictly on a volunteer basis with church or some other ministry, or just informally moving among those people in your circle of influence. No matter what is in store for you regarding this journey, allow for the time that's needed to complete the work God wants to do. You can expect the weeks to become months, and maybe eventually turn into years depending on how much "stuff" you will need to transcend. The whole process for me took a little over four years. No regrets.

"But I don't have the time to take years to get this right!" you might say. That's like the people who really want to finish school and realize it'll take a few years. They say something like, "But I'll be forty before I get my degree." Well, guess what. You'll be forty anyway. Might as well get there with the degree.

Those who don't know their passion or who are not willing to dig for it will be caught up in the flow of life circumstances. They will let life happen to them and end up wherever the flow takes them. That default setting is rarely a recipe for success. Yes, there are those few who stumble onto luck and/or success, but waiting for your ship to come in will result in just that...waiting. Instead of being the "victim" of life's ebb and flow, <u>make something happen</u>!

Start now. Don't wait until a better time. We are only on this earth for a short period. That time is too precious to be shackled by all the hesitations and fears that your mind can harbor. Dig deep for that passion, watch those fears gradually dissipate, and go out there and change some lives!

Our Founders did just that. They were heroes in many ways. They paid a huge price to secure the freedoms that we assume today. How flippantly we say, "I can do what I want, it's a free country." That kind of freedom <u>did not exist</u> before our nation was formed. That kind of freedom and prosperity came only as the result of a <u>huge price paid by people with tremendous passion</u>.

On July 4, 1776, the Declaration of Independence marked the birth of a new nation. The fifty-six courageous men who signed it knew that they might have been signing their death warrant. At best, they were in for a monumental struggle to secure what they had just declared. At worst, they would be hanged for treason. The closing words of this solemn document say it all:

"With a firm reliance on the protection of Divine Providence, we mutually pledge to each other our lives, our fortunes, and our sacred honor."

The fifty-six signers found out what those words would mean over the next several years. Five were captured and tortured by the British before they died. Twelve had their homes sacked, looted, occupied or burned by the enemy. Two lost sons in the army, one had two sons captured. Nine of them died in the war. Many others suffered a myriad of hardships from financial collapse to being a fugitive on the run.

Since then brave men and women have built this country by working in it, fighting for it, and often dying for it. Their passion was the only way they were able to live at such a high level. We dare do nothing less. There is too much at stake.

You will leave a legacy, whatever it may be. Those before us paid the price to establish a nation under God that has the capacity to be not just the "City on a Hill," but to be the instrument that God uses to reach a lost and hurting world. Let us be part of an awakened and passionate populace that does the everyday heroic acts of loving God, our family and neighbors, and giving of our time, talent and treasure to fulfill God's Great Commission in the 21ˢᵗ century.

About the Author

—⟋⟋⟋—

Don Nixon is a thirty-year veteran of Youth for Christ, having begun his career as a member of Southwest PA YFC/Campus Life ministry staff in Washington, PA (1976-84). He was the founding Executive Director of Metro-Pittsburgh YFC (1985-2000) and currently serves as Pennsylvania State Director for the Eastern States Region of YFC. Don graduated from Peters Twp. High School (McMurray, PA) in 1972 and the University of Pittsburgh in 1976.

Don married the former Shileen Keszeg from Newport News, VA in 1983. They have two sons, Justin (19) and Austyn (14) and currently reside in McMurray, just outside of Pittsburgh, PA.

To contact Don Nixon or inquire concerning speaking engagements please call 724-941-7400 or email at yfcpa@ hotmail.com or write to P.O. Box 12931, Pittsburgh, PA 15241. www.donnixon.com

Sources

—ᴍ—

This book is not intended to be a scholarly work. The main desire here is to drive home a stewardship issue that I believe to be of utmost importance to American Christians. Nonetheless, I want to be accurate with the facts. The following sources are listed merely to indicate from where I mined much of the information.

1776 by David McCullough (Simon and Shuster)
America's Christian Roots by Darrell Scott
America's Heritage by Gary DeMar
     (Coral Ridge Ministries)
Barna Report by George Barna (April 25, 2005)
     www.barna.org
Christian History Magazine (issues 33, 45, 50)
God and Ronald Reagan by Paul Kengor (ReganBooks)
Important American Documents by Darrell Scott
Megashift by James Rutz (Empowerment Press)
Original Intent by David Barton (WallBuilder Press)
Oxford Companion to United States History
     edited by Paul S. Boyer (Oxford University Press)
The Rebirth of America (Arthur S. DeMoss Foundation)
Under God by Toby Mac and Michael Tait
     (Bethany House)